WRESTLING SUPERST★RS

BIG SHOW

BY JESSE ARMSTRONG

BELLWETHER MEDIA • MINNEAPOLIS, MN

EPIC

EPIC BOOKS are no ordinary books. They burst with intense action, high-speed heroics, and shadows of the unknown. Are you ready for an Epic adventure?

This edition first published in 2015 by Bellwether Media, Inc.

No part of this publication may be reproduced in whole or in part without written permission of the publisher. For information regarding permission, write to Bellwether Media, Inc., Attention: Permissions Department, 5357 Penn Avenue South, Minneapolis, MN 55419.

Library of Congress Cataloging-in-Publication Data

Armstrong, Jesse.
  Big Show / by Jesse Armstrong.
    pages cm. – (Epic. Wrestling Superstars)
  Includes bibliographical references and index.
  Summary: "Engaging images accompany information about Big Show. The combination of high-interest subject matter and light text is intended for students in grades 2 through 7"– Provided by publisher.
  Audience: Ages 7-12.
  ISBN 978-1-62617-178-7 (hardcover : alk. paper)
  1. Big Show, 1972–Juvenile literature. 2. Wrestlers–United States–Biography–Juvenile literature. I. Title.
  GV1196.B57A75 2015
  796.812092–dc23
  [B]
                         2014034782

Printed in the United States of America, North Mankato, MN.

TABLE OF CONTENTS

WARNING!

The wrestling moves used in this book are performed by professionals.
Do not attempt to reenact any of the moves performed in this book.

THE DEBUT

"Stone Cold" Steve Austin and Vince McMahon battle inside a steel cage. Austin appears in control until the floor rips open. A giant bursts out!

"STONE COLD" STEVE AUSTIN

VINCE McMAHON

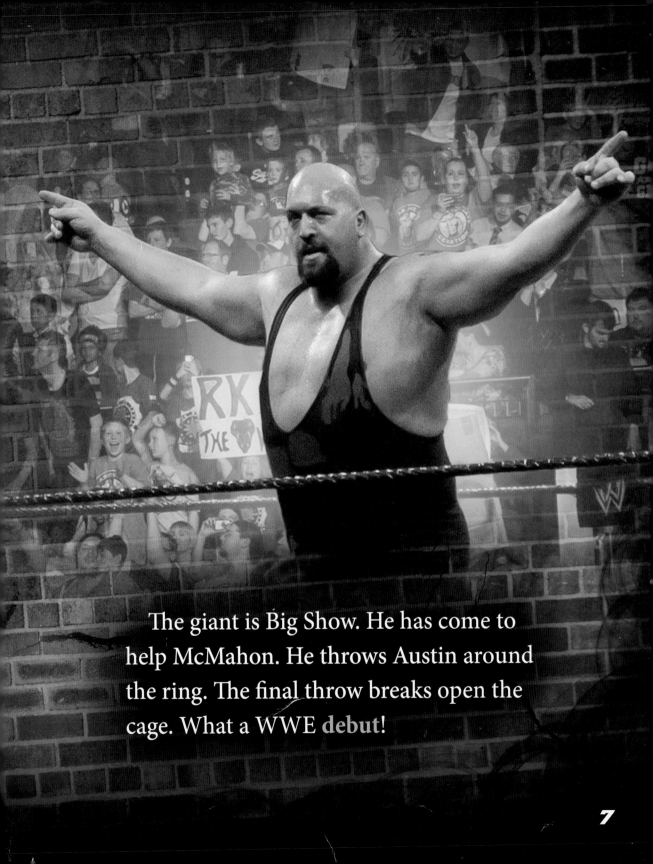

The giant is Big Show. He has come to help McMahon. He throws Austin around the ring. The final throw breaks open the cage. What a WWE debut!

WHO IS BIG SHOW?

Big Show is called the World's Largest Athlete. He stands 7 feet (2.1 meters) tall and weighs more than 400 pounds (181 kilograms). Most opponents cannot measure up.

BIG SHOES
TO FILL

★

His big boots are
a size 22!

LIFE BEFORE WWE

Big Show has been large since childhood. He was born with **acromegaly**. This medical condition caused him to grow fast. He eventually needed surgery to stop growing.

★

Big Show's size made him a star athlete in school. He played football and basketball. Hulk Hogan noticed his size at a basketball event. The superstar encouraged him to wrestle.

HULK HOGAN

A WWE SUPERSTAR

STAR PROFILE

WRESTLING NAME: Big Show

REAL NAME: Paul Wight, Jr.

BIRTHDATE: February 8, 1972

HOMETOWN: Aiken, South Carolina

HEIGHT: 7 feet (2.1 meters)

WEIGHT: 425 pounds (193 kilograms)

WWE DEBUT: 1999

FINISHING MOVE: Chokeslam

In 1995, Big Show debuted in World Championship Wrestling (WCW). At 23, he became WCW's youngest champion. He joined WWE in 1999. Fans first saw him as a heel.

Big Show has feuded with many superstars. But he has formed tag teams with just as many. He has won titles with The Miz, Chris Jericho, and others.

THE MIZ

CHRIS
JERICHO

TEN PLUS

Big Show's title wins
include more than
ten tag team
championships.

17

WINNING MOVES

The KO Punch is one of his **signature moves**. Big Show drives his fist into an opponent's face. The powerful punch knocks his opponent out.

KO PUNCH

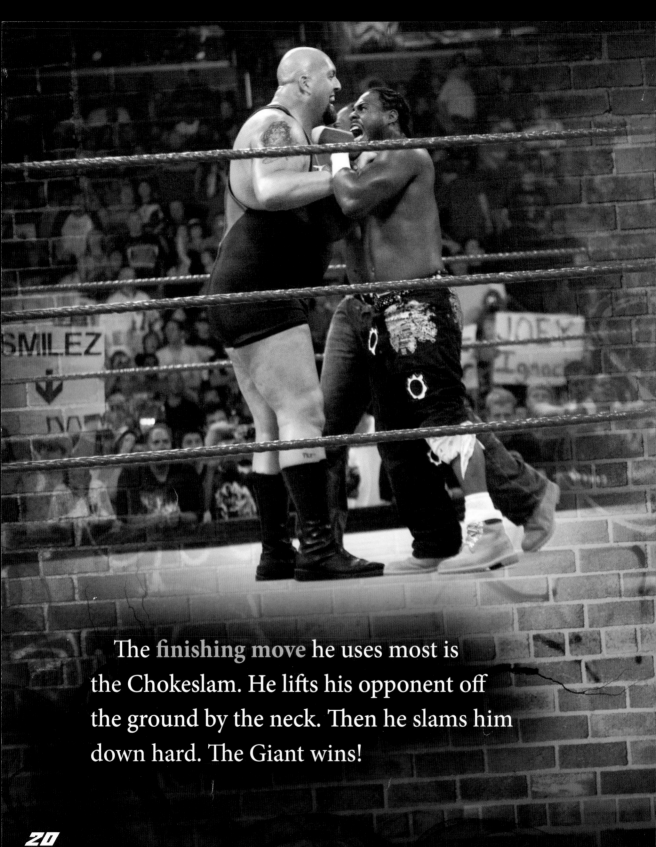

The finishing move he uses most is the Chokeslam. He lifts his opponent off the ground by the neck. Then he slams him down hard. The Giant wins!

CHOKESLAM

GLOSSARY

acromegaly—a medical condition that causes extreme growth

debut—first official appearance

feuded—participated in long-standing, heated rivalries with other wrestlers

finishing move—a wrestling move that finishes off an opponent

heel—a wrestler viewed as a villain

signature moves—moves that a wrestler is famous for performing

tag teams—wrestling pairs that compete as teams

titles—championships

TO LEARN MORE

At the Library

Armstrong, Jesse. *Mark Henry.* Minneapolis, Minn.: Bellwether Media, 2015.

Black, Jake. *WWE General Manager's Handbook.* New York, N.Y.: Grosset & Dunlap, 2012.

West, Tracey. *Race to the Rumble.* New York, N.Y.: Grosset & Dunlap, 2011.

On the Web

Learning more about Big Show is as easy as 1, 2, 3.

1. Go to www.factsurfer.com.

2. Enter "Big Show" into the search box.

3. Click the "Surf" button and you will see a list of related web sites.

With factsurfer.com, finding more information is just a click away.

INDEX